"There minds as content that is ... Christ. But this little book of meditations, drawn from a faithful 19th century pastor, is an antidote for our angry age. *Nearer Heaven* is simple, yet profound, pulling us back toward the love and sacrifice of Christ, toward repentance and reflection, toward holiness and hope. I encourage you to add this resource to your daily quiet time."

Daniel Darling, Senior VP at NRB and author of several books including, *The Characters of Christmas*, *A Way With Words*, and The *Dignity Revolution*.

"It's my joy to recommend this little devotional. Give it a try and I think you'll find it will prove a blessing to you over the next 31 days. Not only that, but you may well find it a resource you return to again and again."

Tim Challies, Challies.com

God is not half-hearted, even though we so often are. This is why *Nearer Heaven* is so important. With each stirring and convicting daily reflection, John Baird provides a pattern for devotional thinking, helping us reflect wholeheartedly on the person of Jesus Christ and doctrinal truths about him and ourselves. Each short entry is packed with honest and biblical insights that re-orient our hearts and minds to find rest and joy in Christ alone. Baird writes with poetic passion, crafting thirty-one devotions that often read like New Testament psalms and proverbs. Readers will be able to revisit this practical and inspiring resource again and again. As we do, the book will shape our prayers, call us to repentance, and urge us to bask in the presence of our gracious God. Indeed, *Nearer Heaven* is true to its name, for that is where it leads us.

Jeremy W. Johnston, columnist, poet, and author of *All Things New: Essays on Christianity, culture & the arts* and *Undiminished Returns: Poems of a Christian Life*.

Nearer Heaven

"If you are ever longing, you are ever praying."
—Augustine

NEARER HEAVEN

*31 daily devotionals for the
deepening of spiritual life*

JOHN BAIRD

EDITED BY
Paul Martin

Nearer Heaven: 31 daily devotionals for the deepening of spiritual life
Edited by Paul Martin

Copyright © 2021 H&E Publishing
www.hesedandemet.com

Source in public domain: John Baird, *Nearer Heaven: A Help to the Deepening of Spiritual Lif*e (London: J. Nisbett & Co. 1884).

Published by: H&E Publishing, Peterborough, Canada

Paperback ISBN: 978-1-989174-92-0
eBook ISBN:978-1-989174-93-7

Contents

Introduction 1
Paul Martin

Preface 3

Nearer Heaven 5

Introduction

It is rare to find a book that both instructs the mind and enflames the soul.

Once, when scavenging through Berdie's Used Goods in Chesley, Ontario, Berdie herself offered me a stack of religious books for free. Nobody else seemed to want them. I scanned through the pile and put *Nearer Heaven* in the "no thank you's." Whether it was the Holy Spirit or simple greed, something prompted me to pick up that worn copy once more and slap it on the top of the "takers." How often I have thanked the Lord for that providential gift!

Of the Rev. John Baird very little is known. The original book was published in 1884 in Edinburgh and it appears from the publisher's advertising our author wrote several other works. His somewhat common name makes searching the historical records all the more difficult since there were a plethora of clergy with the same. There is a reference in the work *Scottish Theology* to a "Mr. John Baird at Paisley" who,

Nearer Heaven

according to one witness, "was one of the worthiest men for learning and piety in his time." Although we cannot be sure that these comments refer specifically to our author, they do offer what we would imagine, from the contents of his writing, a worthy description.

Baird's strength is in packing deep truths into short, pithy phrases. These phrases and small paragraphs betray a profound yet practical theology that thrills the soul with a greater love for the Saviour. In this sense, he has succeeded in his effort to be "like the Psalms," causing our heart to express a whole range of emotion yet somehow never offend or lose sight of our Lord. Whether as a quick read in the rush of life or as a slow meditation in the quiet times, there is always something on which the soul can feed.

It is my prayer that this work, republished so graciously by H&E Publishing, will ignite in all who read it and meditate on the truths it contains, a deeper, more vital relationship with Jesus, our Living Lord who sits at the Father's right hand. For to be nearer to him is to be nearer to heaven.

Paul Martin
Pastor, Grace Fellowship Church
Toronto, Ontario

Preface

This book is intended for private devotional use—to assist our fellowship with God, to deepen our consciousness of Jesus, to suffuse our natures with the spirit of the better world. Following the example of the Psalms, the breathings are general in their character, and aim at expressing the varying conditions, longings, and needs, of spiritual experience.

It is of vital importance for personal holiness, that we cultivate the devotional spirit. One of the great dangers to be guarded against is, externalism in the Christian life, simply hearing, doing, working and neglecting to foster and deepen that inwardness and spirituality, upon which depend the life of God in the soul. There is with many too little meditation, aspiration, serenity, and communion, repose. But how can they grow if they are not rooted—their hearts planted deep in the Invisible?

The following chapters may be used as morning portions, or thoughts may be selected from them for meditation during the leisure hours, and made the cry of the soul for the day.

May the gracious Redeemer bless them to the promotion of unworldliness of soul, and the deepening of that devotional life, whose longings bring us nearer Heaven.

John Baird
Morningside, Edinburgh
November, 1884

Day 1

Think of Jesus, who was so rich and became so poor, and learn of him humility.

> *"The precious blood of Christ."*
> *1 Peter 1:19*

I cannot erase the memory of my sins; but, O Jesus, I can cling with faith to your atoning sacrifice.

More and more I am feeling it is a blessed truth, that your blood cleanses from all sin.

I can trust my pardon to you without any anxiety or fear. It is the comfort of my heart, that the mercy I need, you will not deny.

I cannot pay you what I owe, and in your grace you do not require me.

Why should I have any doubts of you? My unbelief is without excuse; O, that it were uprooted in my heart!

Nearer Heaven

What am I that I should be so much to you, and you should do so much for me?

You forgive me, but I cannot forgive myself. I stand weeping at your feet like Mary, ashamed of my sins.

When I bring my sins to you in penitence, you will not let me carry any of them away.

You were my sacrifice, bearing my sins, my sicknesses, my needs; and it is when I forget these things, that my soul is troubled.

There is nothing lacking in your salvation to my complete happiness; but there is much lacking in my faith.

The judgment day was once to me a terror; but since I was enabled by your grace to leave my case in your hands, I can think of it with peace.

Day 2

Think of Jesus who inspired his closest associates with reverence, and learn of him so to live that those about you may see nothing in you but holy purity of character.

> *"Cleanse me from secret faults."*
> *Psalm 19:12*

Pardon my repentances, they come so much short of my sins.

When I look into myself I see many secret sins—pride, malice, envy, hatred, selfishness. O, cleanse me from their guilt, and save me from their power.

You, O Jesus, are a discerner of spirits, and you see what terrible lusts and feelings lie in my heart concealed.

I did not know myself till I knew you; and then my best goodness paled before your pure righteousness.

My self-abhorrence has been deep; but, ah! It would be deeper had I a full view of my sins. I fear sometimes to examine myself because of the discoveries I would make, and am too conscious of sin to ask you.

Once I thought that when my life was free from outward offence I would be perfect, but I have learned there are secret springs of evil within, which make me a sinner still.

A time was, O God, when I thought myself holy: alas, it was a dream! For an irritating word was spoken, and it kindled a flame of evil passion within.

There is nothing, O God, of which I ought to be more conscious than my sins; and alas, there is nothing of which I am less!

I come to the fountain, but am not refreshed. I eat bread, but am not satisfied. I read your Word, but do not feel its power. My heart is surely wrong, and wedded to some sin.

When is your time for cleansing me? Your time for making me holy? Your time is always now.

O, that I may feel the sinfulness of the sin of disobeying the leadings of the Holy Ghost.

Day 3

Think of Jesus, who laid down his life for you, and learn not to stop short of the sacrifice of your lives for him.

> *"First gave their own selves to the Lord."*
> *2 Corinthians 8:5*

It is not my gifts, but myself, for which you ask.

If I have the will to be wholly yours, you will give the needed power.

I cannot give up anything for you, without your grace rewarding me sevenfold.

You do not need me, but I need you, and I gain all when I gain you.

Religion is nothing in your eyes without sacrifice, and I can only test myself aright by what I am resigning and suffering for you.

Nearer Heaven

You did nothing for me in a half-hearted way. O, that I did all my work earnestly for you. You would not have me to live a life of duty, but a life of loving service.

My life need not be commonplace or dull; for am I not in this world in your name, to do your work, and to advance Your kingdom in every way? Life has had a new meaning ever since I took you.

It is little I possess, it is little I can give, but what I have I give, O Redeemer, to you. I can claim nothing on the ground of my service or my worthiness: it is in your mercy alone I trust.

I am too critical about the work to which I am called. Sometimes I think it too hard, and sometimes too commonplace, but O, teach me that all is sacred which is done for you!

Is my everything upon your altar? Would that I could say so. The will and the power for this great consecration must come from you.

While I cherished any known sin, I could not invite you to convict me; but now that I have put all known sin away, I can pray, "Search me, O God, and try me and see if there be any wicked way in me."

Day 4

Think of Jesus, who bridged a greater gulf to stoop to us than we can ever do in stooping to the lowest; and learn of him, to treat everyman as a brother, and every sinner as a possible saint.

> *"Who loved me."*
> *Galatians 2:20*

Your love to me! Ah, I think too little of it—so infinite, so transcendent, so visible in your every sorrow.

The united love of all saints to you does not equal your love to me.

Many changes come over my heart—now it is hopeful, now it is sad; but no change comes over your love.

It is bliss to be loved by you and perfection to be like you.

Nearer Heaven

I cannot claim your love to me more than other can claim your love to them; for all have the same place in your holy love, O Christ.

Your love indeed was wonderful; nothing was too much for you to bear.

You have more things against me than for me and yet you do not cast me off.

If I thought more of you and your love I would bring myself oftener to account for my sins.

You are, O Jesus, the Saviour of the sad and you are the Saviour for me.

I am unhappy in my backslidings and I weep over my sins: they are sins against your holy love and redeeming sacrifice. Shame and self-reproach would hold me back from you, but your pleading voice prevails with me to come.

I thought in my blindness I had been seeking for you; but when light dawned on my soul, I saw you had been long seeking for me. The knocking has been more on your side than on mine.

Day 5

Think of Jesus, who after the fatiguing day's toil, retired to commune with his Father and learn of him, to permit no weariness to interfere with the hour of prayer.

> *"I will give you rest."*
> *Matthew 11:28*

Breathe on me your Spirit of holy calm, that I may fret less and trust more.

O Jesus, I am unhappy when I look within to myself, more than I look without to you.

Stay my heart on you, for you are my heart's only resting place. Had I but perfect trust in you I would suffer no disquietude.

Your promises are not my experiences, but it is not because they are not true, but because I have not faith.

Nearer Heaven

Rest comes to my heart when it is fully turned to you. I would know less of anxiety if only I knew more of you.

O, to be so conscious of you and your peace, as to be unconscious of self and its ever changing feelings.

Jesus! I have learned that peace is not to be found in my efforts or in trying by my own power to make myself better than I am, but only by looking to you and relying on you with all my heart.

You speak blessed things to me in your gospel; but, O my Saviour, I confess with sorrow that my life is often a dirge when it ought to be a thanksgiving.

I often feel a sense of misery and know the cause of it and yet I refuse to do what alone can bring me happiness.

You gave me rest of soul when I came to you, but I did not keep it. I forgot that while there was a promise of rest on your part there was required an obedience on my part, and that none could retain it who did not take up your yolk. I did not obey you as I ought, and my rest of soul was lost; but I repented and my rest of soul was found.

Day 6

Think of Jesus, who came not to be ministered to, but to minister; and learn of him, to choose a life of sympathy and service for others.

> *"Touched with the feeling of our infirmities..."*
> *Hebrews 4:15*

I can never have any pains which you did not suffer.

I am never so near your loving heart as when I seem by you to be forgotten.

Where can I better shed my tears than at your sacred feet? You do not always deliver me from my trouble when I cry; and, O Saviour, you are good and wise.

I find nothing so comforts my heart as telling my sorrows to you. O gentle Jesus, you do not judge me harshly or unkindly, but with great compassion.

You are more human than my fellows: you are a truer brother than any son of man.

Nearer Heaven

I often have tears I cannot shed, but you see my weeping.

The contrast of my heart with yours brings me shame; mine is narrow, selfish, cold, but yours is rich in its sympathy, tender in its pity, all-embracing in its love.

In the agonies of my soul no thought was so sweet to me as that you, O Jesus, pitied me.

It is not in my power to do much for you, but you estimate service not by the quantity of the work, but by the quality of the motive; and whatever I do, and however imperfectly I do it, if done sincerely for you, it is pleasing and precious in your eyes.

The things of the world parch my soul and I need ever to be turning to you for a draught from the heavenly springs.

Day 7

Think of Jesus, whom no difficulties turned aside from his purpose, and learn of him with calmness of mind to pursue the mission given you by God.

> *"By your patience possess your souls."*
> *Luke 21:19*

My future is hidden from my eyes, but, O Saviour, it is safe in your hands.

You have not promised us everything we would have desired; but you have done better, you have promised us whatever we require.

We needlessly disquiet ourselves. O, for your faith in the fatherly care and love of God!

When the world seems against us may we remember it was against you. Notwithstanding all trials we feel you have environed life for us with a bright and sunny atmosphere.

Nearer Heaven

The hope of heaven ought to reconcile me to every cross, yet I sinfully murmur and complain.

Looking back on the past with its weariness and sufferings, we wonder we have held on; but you have sustained us and your right hand has been our stay.

O, that we could learn just to do our work and with contentment leave all results to you!

What can I do but bow my will to yours, O God? It is not easy, for then it were no trial: I feel it hard.

Since I believed in Jesus, you see no sin in me to condemn me; but you do see much sinfulness and in love you chasten me.

I waited for Providence to open the door and I waited in vain; but, O God, when I went forward in faith, your Providence opened up the way as I required.

My being blessed or not blessed all hinges on my faith.

Day 8

Think of Jesus, whose good was evil spoken of and learn of him, to expect the misconstruction of your purest motives.

> *"In the world you will have tribulation"*
> *John 16:33*

Your way of love is often a way of darkness, discipline and trial, and I have found it is by these ways you bring me closer to yourself.

Why should I be cast down with tribulation? Have you not taught me that your religion is a religion of suffering and sacrifice, of crosses and self-crucifixion, from first to last?

You mingle many things in my cup, but in faith I would drink whatever you give. May troubles cease to surprise me, seeing there must be a daily carrying of the cross.

Nearer Heaven

My burden is great, but you bore a greater. Life were too much for me if you were not my friend.

You overcame the world; and this is my hope, that I will overcome its trials and difficulties too. Your long-continued discipline to me is good, for it is not one lesson I need but many, I am so slow a learner of spiritual truth.

Your servant Paul said he took pleasure in infirmities. O, when will my heart be so pure and heavenly as to glory in whatever I may suffer for your sake?

You send your ploughshare deep into our hearts, but the furrows you make are where you cast your seed.

I have thought over your dealings and tried to see their meaning and mercy; but, O Father, I can say nothing but that your judgments are unsearchable.

The world is friendly till we begin to want, but it is when we want, that your friendship, O God, begins.

Day 9

Think of Jesus, who came to his own and his own received him not and learn of him to persevere in well-doing without appreciation.

> *"Be faithful unto death"*
> *Revelation 2:10*

There is nothing wounds your heart more than your people's falls.

You often tax our faith, but you do it to make it stronger.

It is no bondage to be bound to you, it is no tax to serve you; your love binds you to us and our love binds us to you.

O, that I realized more I belong to your spiritual Israel, chosen to witness for you.

O, that I felt your smile to be my best reward and that I laboured and suffered in your service, content to remain unnoticed by men.

My life is too much a conflict and too little a victory; give me the joy of those who overcome.

I live in vain unless I live for you.

Your test of human worth is character and you value above all else faithfulness and yet we trifle in nothing so much as in our religion.

O, may we ever feel that our influence is a great gift and a great responsibility and that by very little it may at any time be lost.

We seek to win others to you and yet we often forsake you ourselves.

I am hard on some sins and easy on others, but you would have me to be hard on all.

I had no sooner said that I would trust you utterly, than, O God, you tested me and at once I felt my weakness. I am done with confidence in self; you are my only stay!

O, that I realized what I believed, that your teachings were to me not ideas but realities; not merely thoughts of my mind, but experiences of my heart.

Day 10

Think of Jesus, with his pure and delicate nature, placed amid the world's sins and sorrows and learn of him, to bear with patience the experience of all human ills.

> *"Holy, harmless, undefiled."*
> *Hebrews 7:26*

Forgiveness was my goal as a sinner and my starting point as a saint.

I want to be more than virtuous; I want to be holy. O Saviour of infinite purity, you see me stained with sin, but wash me and I shall be whiter than snow.

I cannot be content with my present attainments when I think of you, the Holy One and undefiled.

I yearn for a religion deep and unspeakable as yours. Your life teaches what all lives were meant for—God and good.

Nearer Heaven

I have holiness, but mine is spotted, while yours is immaculate. O, when shall I be pure before you, you great searcher of hearts!

Once I thought that I must be holy to fit myself for coming to you, but now I know that the sinner must come to you as he is, and that he can have no holiness without first having you.

I speak and think much of sin. I mourn it, I pray about it, but I do not make up my mind that it must and shall be overcome. Did I do that, the battle would be half won.

I deeply desire a holier life; and this, O God, is the work of your Spirit. I feel grateful even for the desire and oh may I do nothing to quench it.

My salvation turned on the submission of my proud heart, and now, O God, I feel my sanctification is doing the same.

I have sometimes been impatient at my slow progress in grace and it has been a comfort to me your teaching is so clear, that I must grow.

Day 11

Think of Jesus, who ever turned to his Father for his blessing and approval and learn of him, in all things to depend on God.

> *"Without me you can do nothing"*
> *John 15:5*

I am conscious of power only when I am conscious of you. I undertake too much for my strength when I undertake anything without you.

I thought when years passed over me and things about me were different, that I should be holy, loving, perfect; but now I see that my need is not this or that, but your presence, your grace, your Spirit.

You are my Redeemer from sin and you are more—even the promise and pledge of every good.

Alas that I am so content with the unholiness of my heart! My evil is deeper than my sins: it is my nature. O do change and sanctify me.

Nearer Heaven

I brought to you the burden of unforgiven sin and you took it away; and now I bring to you the burden of indwelling sin, none but you can take it away.

I am still in bondage to sin and it is when I seek to get free I feel its fetter and my need of your power to deliver.

I tried to make myself holy by effort all my own, but without success, till, putting myself in your hands, I found your virtue came down upon my soul; and then I was made pure.

I am going back in the spiritual life when I begin to have no definite sense of need.

I am often as a lamp which gives no light, but, O Jesus, I would always shine did my soul abide in you.

Day 12

Think of Jesus, who was amongst us as a servant and learn of him, that true greatness consists in being lowly.

> *"I am meek and lowly in heart"*
> *Matthew 11:29*

You would rather that my heart be faint than that it be presumptuous.

I have had my will in many things and I have gained nothing, but lost much.

When I think of my heart and life I marvel at your forbearance, but when I think of your meekness it is all explained.

I often wander far from you but you are the Good Shepherd and follow me in my erring ways.

Praise be to you, Blessed Jesus, that none have in hopelessness to cry, "Oh that I knew where I might find You!" You dwell at the mercy seat and the poorest of sinners may find you there.

My holiness is not much, it is little else than a longing; but you have pronounced those blessed who hunger for it.

O that, when I thought of the sorrows of the world, my heart were touched as yours and that I were able to speak like you in tender accents to suffering and struggling men!

You are not the Friend of the righteous and the worthy: no, you are the Friend of all who need your help.

I longed to be like others who once seemed to me so holy, so divine, and now in aim and character I have become as they, but I am not content. Nothing can ever content me, O Jesus, but being like you.

Your life was one of endurance—you suffered a constant daily strain and with what majesty you bore it all!

Day 13

Think of Jesus, whose joy was in seeking and saving the lost and learn of him, that life's true happiness is in blessing others and finding our center outside ourselves.

"Do you love me?"
John 21:16

I have loved many things better than you, but now, O Jesus, my heart's desire is to love you better than all. Your love is in great measure unanswered and yet you love on.

My love to you is not self-made, it is your precious gift. I asked you to give me this love and you heard my cry.

Though my love to you were seraphic, still would I long to love you more.

The deepest comfort of my heart is not that Heaven is mine, but that you love me.

Nearer Heaven

O, you who redeemed me with untold sufferings, would that I loved you with an untold love!

You feel the coldness and lukewarmness of those who are yours, oh, then, how often I must have wounded your tender heart.

I do not love the pure things of earth less because I love you, but greatly more, for love to you enhances all human love.

Moments of silence are sweet when I feel them uniting my heart to you.

I thought when I believed I would be able to give you something in exchange for your love to me, but now, after years have passed in the Christian life, I feel I can give you nothing. I am still, O Lord, unworthy, insufficient and enfeebled with sin.

How to love you was long a problem to my soul. I prayed, I made resolutions, I tried to excite my feelings and all was of no avail, until, O blessed Jesus, I turned to you and thought of your love to me.

Day 14

Think of Jesus, who prayed for those who crucified him, and learn of him, to forgive those guilty of life's greatest wrongs.

> *"Ask, and it shall be given to you"*
> *Matthew 7:7*

We mock you with our prayerless prayers.

Words are of no account to you; the pure motive, the earnest heart alone prevail.

When I ask in faith you answer; when I ask in insincerity you throw me back upon myself.

I have proved you and found you more than faithful. Sometimes I do not receive what I ask, but you are preparing a better answer for me.

What can I not put into my prayers? You are willing to do in me, and for me, all things if I am only willing they should be done.

Nearer Heaven

I can never despair of myself, or my prayers, while you are the Lamb standing in the midst of the throne.

O, may I ever feel that in asking the least mercy I ask much and can claim nothing!

According to my faith, so have you given me in my prayers. I have received in the proportion I expected. The vessel I bring is the vessel you fill.

I often ask, as if I had never received; and seek for blessing, as if I had never found any.

I have been like those sickly ones who breathe their own breath instead of the fresh air of heaven; and when my soul has lived upon itself, I have become weak and declining, but when I have lived on you, I have grown pure and strong.

Day 15

Think of Jesus, who after being sealed by the Spirit in baptism was tempted, and learn of him to expect the testing of your faith and character after a season of gracious experience.

> *"I have prayed for you."*
> *Luke 22:32*

You bear me on your heart in heaven and pray for me before the throne. Pardon my forgetfulness of your intercessions and of what I owe to them.

I was afraid to believe lest, after confessing you, I would fall away, but I found that when you pardoned me, you implanted a new life within me and gave me the promise and power of victory over sin.

My falls are many and their shame and guilt would keep me away from God were it not for you.

How can I doubt my salvation? You died, you rose, you ascended into heaven and you intercede. You can save to the uttermost. Though you are enthroned in glory, you have lost none of your tenderness, none of your pity and you are the same as when you wept over the city that rejected you.

Temptations have been good for me: they have taught me my weakness, they have developed my strength and, above all, they have given me experience of your upholding power.

I look too much forward or too much back, instead, O God, of presently doing your will and serving you to the utmost of my power.

I have erred in this, that in the spiritual life I have expected failure. Had I believed your word, that you are able to keep me from falling, I should have stood much better than I have done.

Day 16

Think of Jesus, who never broke the bruised reed nor quenched the smoking flax, and learn of him, tenderness to the downcast and despairing.

> *"Blessed are the poor in spirit."*
> *Matthew 5:3*

I feel one of the great difficulties of the spiritual life to be keeping myself humble. I am ever raising myself up and so lose grace as fast as I attain.

Had it not been written that, "A broken and a contrite heart, O God, you will not despise," my sadness and my wretchedness would have still more utterly cast me down.

You have taught me that it is only when I feel myself to be empty, weak, and nothing that I am prepared for the gift of spiritual power.

Nothing would seem easier than to believe your simple Word, but I find nothing more difficult. There is pride of heart beneath my humility and doubts behind my faith.

I prayed for times of blessing and you gave them, but I forgot they were times of great responsibility; and less watchful than I ought to have been, alas, O God I fell!

I do not want to know how high I stand in grace, I only want to have assurance I am safe in Christ; for the knowledge of even a little grace would make me proud, while the knowledge of many faults, alas, O Lord, does not make me humble!

I think your happiest moment on earth, blessed Jesus, must have been when the penitent woman washed your feet with her tears.

I believe all you have revealed; but, O God, I want something more than faith. I want to feel a relish for and delight in your truth, that your Word may be to me sweeter than honey from the honeycomb.

Day 17

Think of Jesus, who comforted the mourning and blessed the needy unsought and learn of him, to go forth to the saving of souls unasked of men.

> *"He is able."*
> *2 Timothy 1:12*

I cannot meet God's requirements, but you met them for me.

I have no complaint against you, all my complaints are against myself. You have done all things well.

When I look to myself I despair of being holy, but when I look to you, hope fills my heart.

You know I am not what I seem, but you will make me better than I even appear to be.

You are my undertaker for all things and what you have done for others, you will do for me and do for all.

I knew not the Saviour I needed when first I believed, but now that I see my vileness and weakness after a different manner, I thank you that you are a Saviour, omnipotent and all-sufficient.

It was an hour of awful darkness when I felt overwhelmed with my lost condition, but it was as the revelation of heaven to my soul when I saw that you were able to save me.

Two things I am growingly feeling: my sinfulness and my inability to deal with it; your sacrifice and your Spirit are all my hope.

When I have you dwelling in my heart, you are a fountain within, whence flow streams of peace and love and grace through my whole being.

The reign of sin in me is doomed. Your cross passed the sentence upon it, and the coming of your Spirit into my heart is the carrying of it into execution.

Day 18

Think of Jesus, who chose a Peter, a James, a John for his disciples and learn of him, that God's will is done through various types of character.

"By grace are you saved."
Ephesians 5:2

Salvation, O Christ, is your gift: even our perfect holiness could not save us.

O, to grasp the thought of your finished work and to realize with growing clearness that the work is done that saves.

What could equal your graciousness, O Jesus? It is an amazing thought that a humble coming to you is followed by a present, full and everlasting salvation. Your gospel is good news indeed.

You have answered for us the greatest of all questions: "How shall sinners be just with God?"

Nearer Heaven

We are slow to bring our minds to the thought of salvation by grace, eternal life for nothing, but our feeling of helplessness brings us at last.

Your way of salvation is not a new life, then a new heart; but first a new heart and then a new life. In our worldly wisdom we are ever reversing the order.

We are prone to draw distinctions where you draw none; but, O Saviour, we all need the same repentance, the same forgiveness—Nicodemus and the woman of Samaria alike.

One thing I pray to abide with me clear—the consciousness that I am redeemed, that my guilt has been completely taken away in Jesus and that henceforth I am a son of God. O, may the certainty ever possess me that there is now an enduring peace and that nothing can undo the blessed fact of redemption. You do not need, gracious Saviour, to die again; your death was enough once for all.

Though I had only one sin to be forgiven, my debt would be infinitely more than I could pay.

Day 19

Think of Jesus, in whose life there is no trace of worry and learn of him, to commit everything to God.

> *"O you of little faith."*
> *Matthew 16:8*

We hunger when we might be feasting: we long when we might be satisfied.

I come to you with my cares, but instead of casting them on you, I just bring them away.

You might well ask me, as you asked your disciples, "Where is your faith?" For, alas, O Lord, I am anxious when I ought to be calm and I fear when I ought to hope.

My faith ought to grow with difficulties, but you know it generally becomes less.

Fretfulness is foolish and strong faith in you is its only cure.

Nearer Heaven

Your Word speaks of joy, but I do not have it; and of peace as a river, but I do not know it. To what pastures you would lead me if I would only follow you! But ah, I am self-willed; and though you have directed me to look to you I continue looking to myself.

My experience has many phases, but it is a deep well of comfort that nothing can separate me from your love. Life with all its changes would I feel to be joyful were I only consenting to do your will, as in all things the best.

I complain of weakness, but I know it is because I have not continuous trust that I have not continuous spiritual power.

Whatever my sins, if I am only penitent, you will be merciful. You do not ask me, "How much have you sinned?" but, "Are you contrite?" You will forgive me my sins though they be many, if I am penitent. You will not forgive me though my sins be few, if I am not broken-hearted.

Though you are my Father, I often distrust you as though you did not care for your children at all.

Day 20

Think of Jesus, who never compromised with the world and learn of him, to stand fast against all that is against God.

> *"I find then a law, that when I would do good, evil is present with me."*
> *Romans 7:21*

Ah, Lord, the conflict between the flesh and the spirit is no dream. I feel it sadly real. I aspire after the pure and holy and find myself bound as by a chain to sin.

Good and evil will not reconcile and yet I am daily attempting it in life.

O Jesus, it is too true that I cling to the very sins from which I pray you by your grace to deliver me.

My goodness is unstable, my will is inconstant, I am too changeable to be near perfection.

Sin is still in me, O Jesus, but praise be to you it is no more supreme. The more conscious I have become of you, the more conscious I have become of the evil within me.

Sin is more refined in its manifestations since I believed. I would not now do the deeds or say the things I once did, but I feel that what is within me is still sin, which would lead me astray much as it did before. Sin, I see, cannot change, it must be taken away.

I find I can keep myself more easily from open, than from secret sins and that secret sins are my serious temptation.

My complaint is not that I am in the world, but that the world is in me. I cannot get it out of my heart except as I let in you.

You had a faultless life, but I have not a faultless day.

You have, O God, been revealing sin to me more and more and had I seen it, when seeking my Saviour, as I see it now, I could not have sought him at all; but with deeper discoveries of sin, you are granting me richer discoveries of your mercy and I feel no despair.

In my moments of greatest thoughtfulness, I think worse thoughts of myself than my greatest enemy can think of me.

Day 21

Think of Jesus, who lived so near to God and learn of him, however changing your life, to dwell under the shadow of the Almighty.

> *"Abide in me."*
> *John 15:4*

My truest fellowship is with you, for you come closest to my heart.

O, that prayer were to me true converse with you—life's sweetest joy and the heart's holiest delight.

My life is so hurried I do not give you time to speak. Yet how much you have to say to my soul.

O, for the heart that comes to you not to ask favours, or urge further blessings, but that delights to abide with you out of a pure love for your presence!

When I enjoy fellowship with you, my heart has no desire for fellowship with the world.

Nearer Heaven

More and more I feel that the only way to be strong is to wait on you.

I sometimes rest more on what you have done than on what you are in yourself; but oh for the faith that rises to your person!

Gracious Redeemer, will you not lead me up to some transfiguration mount and show me your glory?

My life is lived on a common level, when it might be lived in the heavenly places with you.

I cannot enjoy you if I am not entirely yours. I have only been half-hearted for you; and I know not the deeper joys that are given your own.

When you forgive us, you admonish us: "Go and sin no more."

How glorious are the privileges of the spiritual life—the privilege of being yours, of following you, of communing with you, and glorifying your holy name. It is because I dwell on these privileges so little that I think of my difficulties so much.

Day 22

Think of Jesus, who never lost his charity and learn of him, to be generous to all and generous to the last.

> *"I in them and you in me."*
> *John 17:23*

I do not realize my union with you as I ought. I think too much of myself as another and not as one with you.

What can deliver me from my sinful self? I feel that the secret of holiness is not example, nor education, nor experience, nor my efforts, nor my prayers, but your Spirit dwelling in my heart.

You are in me by your Spirit; oh, lead me to a greater love of the Spirit, a greater thankfulness for his presence and a greater recognition of his work.

The story of your love, your sacrifice and the shame and grief you bore, even these did not convert me; my hard heart needed your Spirit to melt it and bring it under conviction of sin.

Nearer Heaven

Surely, O Lord, there are experiences beyond what I yet know. I have not your Spirit so dwelling within me and so quickening and refreshing my heart, as a well of water springing up to everlasting life.

You promised another Comforter and your Spirit is a Comforter indeed; for it so fills my songless heart with emotions, that it bursts into voice.

Many impressions, very solemn and very pleasing, have passed quite away, which I thought might abide. But had they remained, O God, I might have made my feelings my Christ.

The more I look into Your life, the more I see what mine should be.

Day 23

Think of Jesus, whose ideal of man was so high and yet whose contact was with men so low and learn of him, as you move among the outcast and degraded, to feel that one soul is more than the world and that even for the worst he died.

> *"We live unto the lord."*
> *Romans 14:8*

O, for more true love to you and your work—more burning desire to lead sinners to yourself—more heavenly wisdom in dealing with immortal souls!

I am often selfish in my aspirations. I long for the enjoyment of certain pleasing inward feelings, rather than for being made and used as an instrument for your glory.

I have no greater need than pure motives in all I do for you.

Nearer Heaven

Your gospel teaches us that there are higher and more Christlike things than personal comfort and a feeling of spiritual well-being, even the giving away of ourselves more completely in sacrifice for you.

How blessed is the work of pointing sinners to you; may it be the meat and drink of our souls, more and more!

My worldly estate prospers and my comforts abound. I have all I can desire; but, O God, no satisfaction is so pure and deep as encouraging, blessing and edifying the souls of my fellow men.

I am apt to lean more on my own efforts than on your blessing, but unless you give the increase all labour is for naught.

I pray that you would do with me as you will; but when you do so, how prone I am to complain.

I have three great needs that I may go forth to your work aright—the spirit of gladness, the spirit of hopefulness, the spirit of consecration.

I am finding it difficult to go through this world wisely. I am silent when I ought to speak and I speak when I ought to be silent. My life is full of mistakes in words and actions.

Day 24

Think of Jesus, who did no meaningless things, who passed no idle days and learn of him, to live lives full of earnest purpose.

"The brightness of the father's glory."
Hebrews 1:3

We find God when we find you. We have received many gifts but you are the greatest gift of all.

We are seeing more in you than we once saw and we are feeling more of your gracious power; but, O, how inadequate are our thoughts and experience still! We would gaze on you till we feel the rays of your glory streaming forth from your person on our souls.

We cannot find a fault with you even if we would. Preserve us from all irreverence towards you and may we never forget what is due you because of your great majesty.

Nearer Heaven

Lead us up to the high heights of divine experience and let the revelation of your glory shine upon our souls.

We drink of the streams of earthly happiness, but, O Jesus, we thirst again. Our hearts desire what this world cannot yield.

When in the hour of death all earthly objects fade from vision, may your cross stand out vividly before my eyes.

I often ask myself, why I am in the world? What is the purpose of my being? Does the grave end all? Are the yearnings of my heart nothing? Was I born merely to die? All, O Jesus, had been mystery and darkness without you; but you have brought life and immortality to light.

We see your power, O God, in creation, but not yourself. It is only Jesus who has shown us you.

As I live near to you, I grow more conscious of my defects and more sensible of your perfections.

Day 25

Think of Jesus, so compassionate in his dying hour, and learn of him, to be mindful of others, even while you may be suffering yourselves.

"Who gave himself for me."
Galatians 2:20

Father, I do not wonder at your anger against sin, for you are holy and you are just. The sacrifice of your dear Son is no strange faith to me, for I feel I need his precious blood; my heart craves for an atoning Saviour. It is a mystery, blessed Jesus, that you came; but having come, it is no mystery that you died.

I fear not, O Christ, to think I have sinned, for I know that you have died.

I have tried excuses with myself, but my best excuses bring me no real peace. After all my reasoning, O God, an uneasy secret conviction remains. Nothing

Nearer Heaven

but your absolving and peace-speaking Word can give me peace.

Some have spoken much to me of faith, but there is a deeper need—the broken heart. Without it, how can I believe and yield myself to your grace? With it, I cannot but believe and surrender to your call.

Saviour, bless me, that is my prayer. I ask not for greater earthly good, or better health, or other friends—I leave all my life to you. Arrange, withhold, and give as you see best.

When I fill up my days with work for you, I find life to be not a burden but a boon!

I could not live as I do if I realized the greatness of your redeeming love and sacrifice.

You have hourly cleansing for my hourly sinfulness, and as often as I come to you, you make me pure.

Day 26

Think of Jesus, who rebuked Simon and approved Mary, and learn of him, that it is love he values above all else in man.

"If any man thirst let him come to me and drink."
John 7:37

You know what is in man and you love him. But a keen perception of human character on our part makes us misanthropic, for we see so much that is unsatisfactory, disappointing and mixed in each, that we are tempted to spurn all. We need your love to make us loving and your Spirit to make us human.

It is not my intellect, or the government of my life by prudence, by thoughtfulness, or by wise concern that makes me spiritual, but only the inhabitation of my heart, by your Spirit, O God. Without your Spirit I would be carnal however my mind were cultured and refined.

Nearer Heaven

A deep error runs through my life; I treat the little things of time as great and the great things of eternity as little. I feed on husks when I might feed on you, the Bread of Life the Manna of the soul.

I never rightly knew you, till in my extremity I made proof of you.

You have not changed since you were on earth and your fullness of blessing is the same.

You do not represent the spiritual life as so difficult to live and yet I find it so; and it is, O Lord, because I have not given myself fully up to you.

My way, O God, is from blessing to rise to trust; but your way is, from trust to rise to blessing. Teach me to be less anxious about receiving blessing and more anxious about resting in you as faithful.

Day 27

Think of Jesus, whose supreme ideal was goodness and learn of him, that moral worth is the true dignity and the highest excellence of man.

"Christ is all and in all."
Colossians 3:11

It has taken me long to attain a spirit of entire dependence. But years and trials and varied experiences have brought me to a sense of nothingness. I feel the Christian life different since I reached it. It is more a reality, a victory and a joy.

The spiritual change within me has been divinely and not personally wrought. I would not be what I am but for your grace.

And now I do not glory in what I am, but in what you are and what you have been to me. I seek the greater graces, when it would be better if I practiced the lesser virtues. I cannot be perfectly holy, if I am imperfectly human.

I give up the world, the flesh, the devil. I resign all that has been most dear, not, O Jesus, that you may love me, but because you have loved me.

Now that you are so precious to me, I wonder I ever preferred anything to you.

I am far from counting all things but loss—it is a humbling confession to make, but you know it is true. I have not yet fully learned the first lesson of your gospel, which is to leave all things for you.

You have repaired all losses by the fall and more; your redemption is a greater remedy than our disease. Sin has abounded, but your grace has much more abounded.

I have often prayed for feeling, when I ought to have prayed for faith. When I have believed in you aright, the feelings I desired have come.

It is one thing, O Christ, to read your Word, it is another to listen to your voice.

Day 28

Think of Jesus, who blessed the world by the example and sacrifice of a life lived for God, and learn of him, that while to advance the world by science and discovery is honourable, and can only be the lot of the few, it is a higher vocation to enrich it by holiness, which lies within the power of all.

> *"He that abides in me and I in him,*
> *the same brings forth much fruit."*
> *John 15:5*

Some are asking, "How may your work be better done?" I feel I shall never do it better than now, without a more sanctified personal character. Man's solution is new schemes and methods, but your solution is a higher type of life and a deeper tone of piety.

I say to myself, I am forgiven; but Lord, you teach me that that is not enough; for you addressed the condemning language, "You wicked and lazy slave," not to one who had done evil, but to one that had done no good.

What in my pride I hated, that in your providence you have sent. What I once scorned the thought of having to do, that, O God, I have had to do. Your discipline has broken my will.

I will not be wholly yours until I am able to do or suffer anything for your sake.

I would, O Jesus, as I stand beneath your cross, see your wounds and gaze upon your agony, till I feel I can never sin against you again and that to die were better than to live without your favour, your fellowship, your smile.

My outward work often goes beyond my inward grace, but all true zeal in your eyes is the outcome of the inner life. Alas, it is my mistake that I am more taken up with my service than I am with my Saviour!

The life of my soul, instead of burning as a flame, sometimes dies down to a spark; and then my only comfort is that you will not break the bruised reed or quench the smoking flax.

Day 29

Think of Jesus, who after accepting the will of his Father in Gethsemane was prepared for all his sufferings and learn of him, that complete surrender is the secret of acquiescence.

> *"Overcame by the blood of the lamb."*
> *Revelation 12:11*

You gave me power, O God, to come to Jesus, but I need power to live near him. I am unequal to a spiritual life, without daily supplies of grace. My many falls have taught me my weakness.

My heart has its times of deadness, when even the thought of Jesus brings me little sensible comfort, and yet I cannot doubt I am yours. I can trust your faithfulness that I am safe. You are teaching me by these experiences to look away from myself and to rest my faith in Jesus, my atoning sacrifice.

Nearer Heaven

I would not be as I am if I lived as I ought, upon my Saviour's fullness.

Your Gospel is not that since I believed I may be saved, but that I am saved. O, make it clear to my soul that there is no condemnation for me now.

It is not because I once came to you I believe I am saved, but because I have always been coming and come now to you again.

A great barrier in the way of my holiness is just the unwillingness of my soul to be entirely yours.

I seem never to be out of conflict, but I take comfort from the thought that if I were on Satan's side, he would not trouble me so much.

Penitence is deepening in my heart and I am beginning to feel that my least sin as a saint is greater than my greatest sin as a sinner.

O Jesus, send Your mercy down upon me: it is healing balm to my wounded heart.

Day 30

Think of Jesus, infinitely tender in his heart, yet infinitely strong in his character and learn of him, to blend majesty and meekness in daily life.

> *"Lo, I am with you always."*
> *Matthew 28:20*

I have not seen you with my eyes, but I have felt you in my heart.

Much has been given me—your Word, your church and all the blessings of your salvation—but these blessings are not yourself.

However poor we be, with you we are rich; and however rich we be, without you we are poor.

I am more anxious about having peace and joy than about having you; but teach me, O Christ, you are my great possession.

You are near, ever near, and the briefest word of prayer brings me to your feet.

Nearer Heaven

It is a small part of my life that meets the human eye, my great life is imperceptible and only lived before you.

You know, O Jesus, the pain, the agony of losing the sense of God. Pilate wronged you, false witnesses accused you, the soldiers scourged you, the weight of the cross oppressed you, the mockers mocked you and you did not open your mouth; but when God forsook you, you broke silence and cried out; and what the presence of your Father was to you, your presence is to us.

Prayer and life and all things are dull when I do not feel you near.

I was not long saved before I found myself like your people of Israel after their deliverance from Egypt, face to face with difficulties; my old sins coming upon me and nothing but dangers and darkness before me; I knew not where to turn nor how to escape, but your voice spoke to me, "Go forward!" And as I obeyed in faith, the perils vanished and you made a path for me through the waters.

Day 31

Think of Jesus, who, on the mount of temptation, was offered the kingdoms of the world for an act of momentary homage, and learn of him, it is better to forego the world's greatest prizes than be guilty of a single sin.

> *"In my father's house are many mansions."*
> *John 14:2*

Day by day I would raise my heart above, and by your grace keep it there.

I cannot gaze upon your glory, but I can think of it.

I sometimes take dark views of life and death and the future; but, O Jesus, teach me there is before me light and love and blessedness in your Father's house for evermore.

Heaven will be home to me, for you are there. It will have much to reveal, but yours will be the greatest revelation of all.

Nearer Heaven

I do not fear life's last hour, for you will let me lean on you when I come to die and in your bosom I will die in peace.

It is a sweet consolation that I have a home on high beyond life's trials and changes. This is my faith, O God, that all things will come right at last.

I am passing hence, but I am passing hence to you. I could not face eternity without you as my Forerunner and Friend.

Vanity is written on all earthly things and every trial you are sending me is teaching me so.

I do not live upon the future with its blessedness and its glories, but upon you, O Christ, my bread of life.

I once thought of heaven as a place far beyond, but I have learned to look for it in my soul. I must first find it here, before I can find it there.

Nearer to Jesus, Nearer to Heaven

Date Completed	Name

CPSIA information can be obtained
at www.ICGtesting.com
Printed in the USA
BVHW041143070322
630818BV00012B/340